Forex Trend Trading

A Practical Guide to Master the Act of
Trend Trading for Long Term Consistent
Profit

Abraham Robert. C

In order to say thank you for purchasing this book, I offer the below video course and more to you as a token of appreciation

Find the Link to the bonus video courses at the end of the book

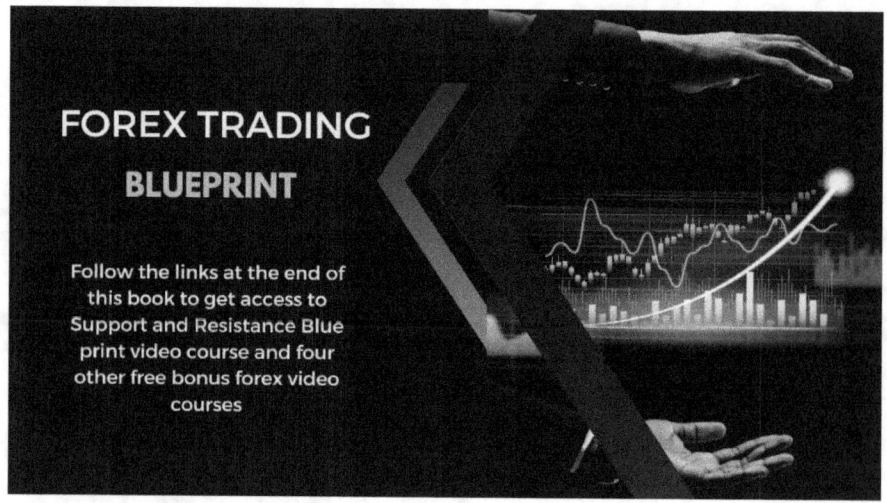

TABLE OF CONTENT

CHAPTER ONE

TREND OVER-VIEW

The overall direction of the price of an asset on the market is called a trend. Any financial instrument's chart will show you that prices seldom move in straight lines; instead, they are made up of a sequence of highs and lows. Prices typically have an upward or downward tilt.

A market trend is the direction of an asset's price over a specific time frame. All assets and markets, including foreign exchange, commodities, stocks, and bonds, whose prices and trade volumes vary, are subject to market movements.

Forex trading trends provide you the chance to recognize the strong market direction and place an order appropriately. Technical analysis is another tool that trend trading uses to help you forecast future price changes.

Trends are defined as the average change in the exchange rate of a currency pair over a given time period. An uptrend is observed when there is a consistent upward movement in the exchange rates of the currency pair; a downtrend is observed when there is a downward movement.

When the forex market has been moving in the same direction for an extended period of time, a shift in trend takes place. A currency pair that has been gradually rising in value under such circumstances begins to decline in value, indicating a shift in the current trend in the direction of a downward trend.

You may recognize a trend with the use of trend trading tactics. By examining the closing price, opening price, and the range that the currency pair has been trending inside, one may ascertain the direction of the trend.

An upward trend is indicated if the trading range of the currency pair is on the high-value side. In this instance, market prices are always rising. When there is an uptrend with higher highs and higher lows, you can enter a long position.

Likewise, a downtrend is indicated if the range is on the low-value side. In this instance, market prices are consistently declining. When there is a downtrend with lower highs and lower lows, you can take a short position.

Additionally, there are times when the market stays in between a high and low level. When the market stays at one price level for an extended length of time, it is referred to be a sideways trend. This means that although short-term traders use sideways trends to their advantage in order to profit from short-term moves, long-term traders should hang onto their current holdings.

A market trend is the direction in which prices have moved over a specific time frame. All assets whose prices are varying or whose trading volume is changing are subject to trends.

In the context of Forex and other financial markets, a trend is commonly defined as a price movement that has a distinct direction and strength and is produced within a specific timeframe. The essential feature of market trends is direction, which traders utilize to guide their actions and optimize profits.

The fundamentals of technical trend analysis state that there are always specific guidelines that apply to price fluctuations.

Because of this, traders who are successful can examine the recurring patterns in the prices of currencies and other market instruments. It is feasible to trade on financial markets using currencies and other investments, predict future asset prices, and make wise trading selections because of the systemic nature of price chart movements. A experienced trader can utilize a plethora of indicators, advisors, and visual patterns within technical analysis. The idea of a price movement is the foundation for the majority of these technologies.

CHAPTER TWO

DIFFERENT TYPE OF TREND

Rising Trend

Bull market tendencies refer to periods of rising prices. A sequence of escalating price highs and lows serves as its representation. The uptrend continues as long as each new peak is higher than the ones that came before it.

In the Forex market, an upward trend indicates a positive trend. This suggests that a currency's value would rise steadily over time. There will thus be higher troughs following peaks and higher peaks following troughs.

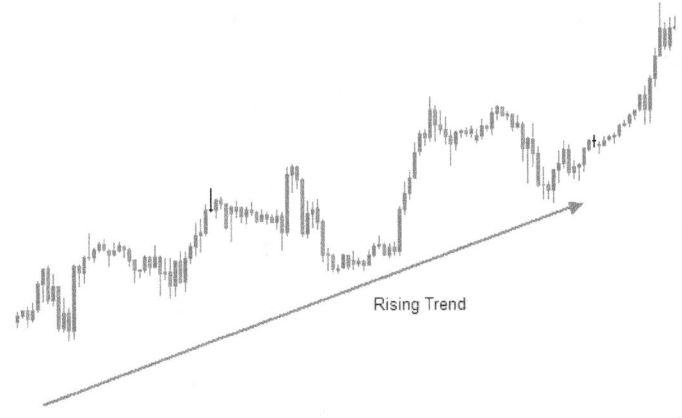

Rising Trend

Drawing a straight line between more than two consecutive low prices may be used to validate a Forex upward trend line as a price trend. An upward trend line is produced by adjoining two subsequent low prices. Put differently, on a trading chart, a trend line is invariably drawn below the geometric patterns formed by price movements.

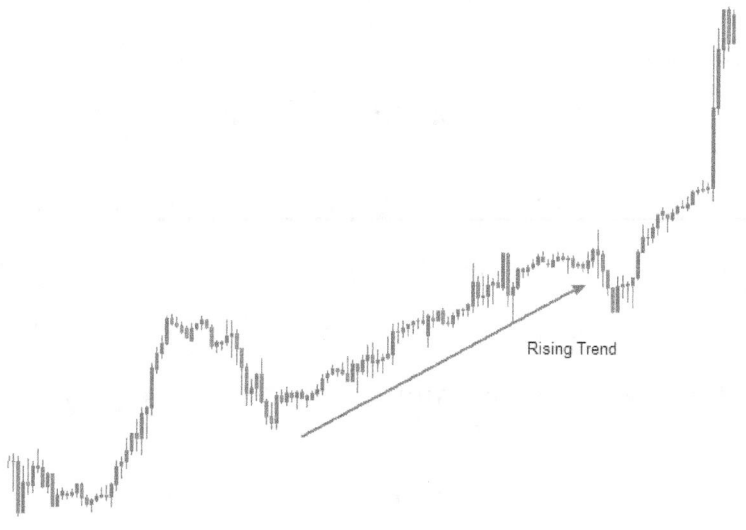

Rising Trend

Declining Trend

Trends in the bear market, or downward market trends, occur when prices decline. Any failed effort to break through the prior high indicates a trend reversal ahead of time. A downtrend is distinguished by a sequence of low points and high points.

Declining Trend

A downtrend in the forex market is characterized by price decreases, which are typically followed by partial consolidations or moves in the opposite direction of the trend. A downward trend indicates that the downward movement will continue, although it does so at a slower rate over time than an upward trend.

In terms of trend analysis, the price graph's lower peaks and valleys are indicative of a downturn. Finding two or more successive highest highs of the ensuing price movement forms a bearish trend line in forex.

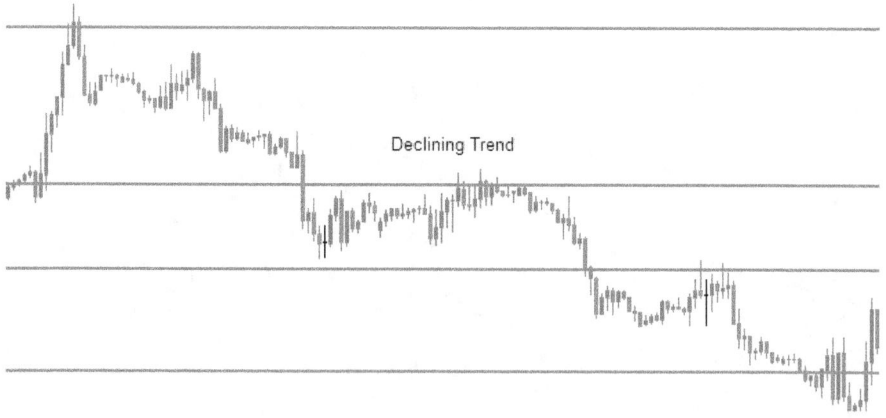

Declining Trend

Consolidation Or Sideways Market

The absence of a strong one-direction movement is known as a sideways (flat) market, and it is a normal and common market state.

A sideways trend in trend analysis is defined as a horizontal price movement between support and resistance levels. It happens when the market lacks direction and frequently consolidates. According to a study of forex trends, the market moves sideways 80% of the time. Professional traders concentrate on the 20% of the time when the market moves in a certain direction. Put simply, "Your profits increase along with a trend."

Side Way Market

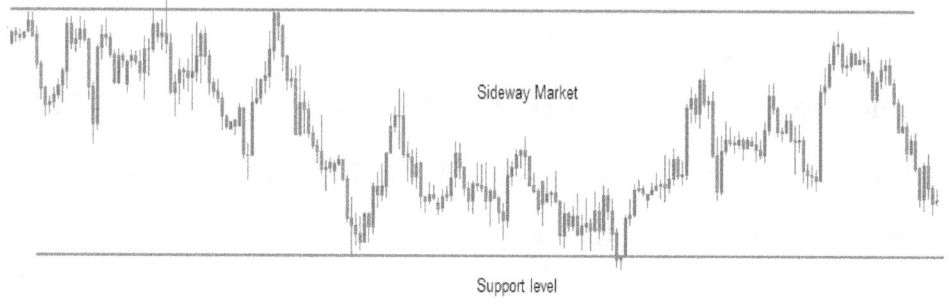

Resistance level

Sideway Market

Support level

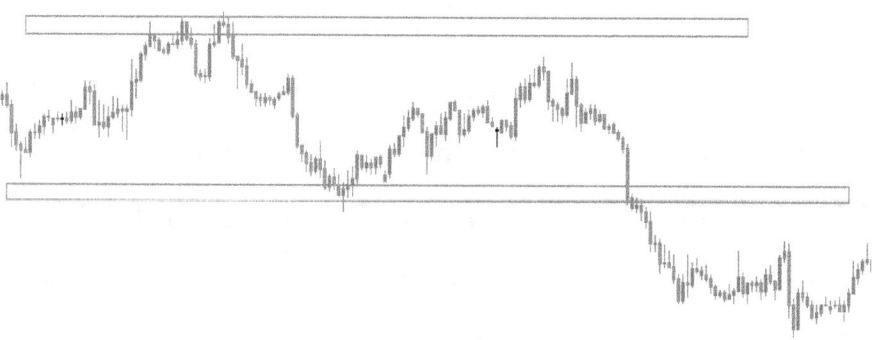

Horizontal lines connecting declines and falls in the currency rate indicate a sideways trend. When the trend ends, which might happen after a few days or even weeks, the price changes. The currency price will often return to its previous direction following a sideways trend in the market.

Trends can vary in duration and it includes:

Major Trend

Major (long-term) might span anything from a few months to several years.

Intermediate

Intermediate (secondary, medium-term) trends often indicate a one-to-six-month reversal of the primary trend.

Short Term Trends

A correction or consolidation that lasts less than a month is sometimes referred to as a short-term trend (minor). It could represent a break in a major or intermediate trend. It is also possible to see short-term patterns on intraday charts.

CHAPTER THREE

FACTORS THAT AFFECT TREND

Government Regulations

Governments can influence the growth of market trends by implementing changes to their fiscal and monetary policies. A nation's economic development, for instance, might be impacted by changes in a central bank's interest rate, which would directly affect the defensive and cyclical sectors of the economy.

The US government may affect the value of the US dollar relative to other currencies via a number of different strategies. The Federal Reserve (Fed), the country's central bank, is a separate branch of the government. When the fed funds rate, which is the cost for banks to lend to one another, rises or falls, it indirectly affects exchange rates.

For instance, if the Fed cuts its rate, the U.S. banking system's interest rates also drop, and the money supply rises. Given the expected pressure on inflation, this tends to make the dollar weaker against other currencies. Additionally, the lower rates often result in less demand for assets denominated in dollars, which can negatively impact the value of the currency.

Another government organization that has an indirect impact on currency rates is the Treasury Department. It produces more currency. The dollar is depreciated by this printing, which raises supply. It can also take out more loans from other nations. This is accomplished by selling Treasury notes, which raises the money supply and the amount of debt owed by the United States, both of which depress the value of the dollar.

Using expansionary fiscal policies is the third weapon available to the government. Because they increase the amount of money in circulation, these measures often weaken the dollar.

But these measures can also spur economic expansion, which draws both domestic and international capital to assets denominated in dollars. This demand frequently eclipses the growth in the dollar supply.

Market Sentiment

Every trader will have a different personal theory on why the market is moving in a particular direction.

In trading, dealers convey their opinions in each transaction they make.

However, there are situations where a trader may lose money despite being very certain that the markets will move in a specific way and having all of the trend lines line up nicely.

It is important for a forex trader to understand that the collective viewpoints, concepts, and beliefs of all market participants contribute to the overall market.

Market sentiment is the collective emotion that players in the market experience.

The notion or dominant feeling that the majority of the market believes best explains the market's present trajectory.

The attitude of market participants might influence market developments. A bullish trend may be shaped by traders' and investors' positive view when they believe that a country's economy or a company's business prospects will improve. On the other hand, traders' pessimistic views about the market may cause the asset's price to decline.

Demand And Supply

Market changes are primarily driven by supply and demand. Demand is the quantity of goods and services that are being purchased; supply is the quantity of products and services that are available for purchase.

The dynamics of supply and demand influence the behavior of buyers and sellers in a variety of markets, including daily consumer products and financial ones like shares, currency, and commodities.

Prices will fluctuate if supply and demand are out of balance. When demand outpaces supply, there is a shortage of the thing, which drives up prices since buyers must outbid one another to get the item. On the contrary hand, when supply exceeds demand, there is an excess. Prices decrease as a result of consumers using less of the product or buying alternatives to save money.

The price of an asset often varies in response to changes in the dynamics of supply and demand. This is particularly true for goods. For instance, when the economy is doing well and there is a greater demand for crude oil, oil prices usually rise. Wars and mining interruptions limit supply, which raises costs as well.

Business And Financial News

An upswing might be fueled by encouraging corporate quarterly reports or better-than-expected economic statistics. Negative news, on the other hand, can cause prices to decline and start a downward trend.

Important note

Easily spotting trends in charts involves examining the highs and lows of the data. In this case, an uptrend denotes a sequence of higher highs and higher lows for the price.

CHAPTER FOUR

THE IDEA BEHIND TREND TRADING

How To Identify a Market Trend

To determine market trends, one might employ technical analysis as well as fundamental analysis.

Trendlines, price action, the Relative Strength Index (RSI), and moving averages (MA) are prominent technical analysis tools among traders.

Trendline

A trendline is a straight line that stretches into the future and links a range of price points, including highs and lows.

A support level for upcoming price movements is created by an upward trendline joining a sequence of higher lows. The support level, on the other hand, is indicated by a downtrend trendline linking a sequence of lower highs.

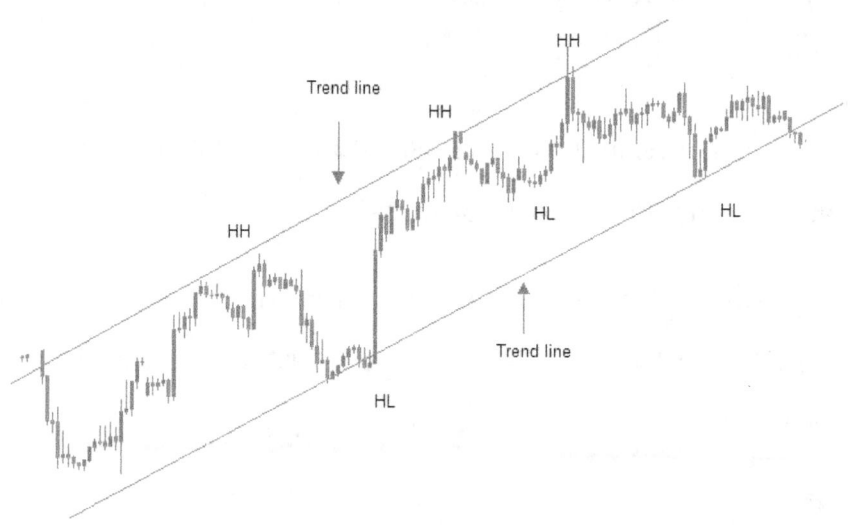

Relative Strength Index (RSI)

An RSI measures the rate and magnitude of price movements to identify if a particular commodity is overbought or oversold.

When the RSI is 30 or lower, the market is considered oversold; when it is 70 or above, the market is considered overbought. These two measurements suggest that a trend reversal is probably imminent.

Moving averages (MA)

Moving averages, meanwhile, are employed to separate discernible price movement from noise in the market. Simple moving average (SMA) and exponential moving average (EMA) are the two types of moving averages.

SMA determines the average price of a group of prices over a predetermined amount of historical time. SMA, for instance, computes the average price over the previous 20, 50, 100, and so forth days. On the other hand, the EMA is a weighted average that highlights the price of a market in the last few days, making it a more sensitive indicator to fresh data.

Moving averages are also utilized to ascertain the general price trend and the levels of support and resistance for an asset's price.

Fundamental analysis

Fundamental analysis can also be used by investors to spot market trends by observing shifts in economic or business indicators like sales and profits growth.

A corporation is an example of a good market trend when its profits growth is positive for many quarters in a row. Conversely, a negative trend is seen when a company's earnings decline over a certain period of time.

In contrast to technical analysis, which is scouring charts for patterns or trends, fundamental analysis entails scouring news headlines and economic data reports. (And even sporadic tweets prior to his suspension from a specific global leader.

By examining the political, social, and economic factors that might have an impact on currency values, fundamental analysis offers a perspective on the foreign exchange market.

It is simple to use supply and demand as a predictor of future prices. Analyzing every aspect that influences supply and demand is the difficult part.

You must comprehend how and why specific occurrences, such as a rise in the unemployment rate, impact a nation's monetary policy and economy, which in turn impacts the degree of demand for its currency.

This kind of research is based on the notion that a country's currency should appreciate if its economic prospects are favorable, both now and in the future.

Foreign companies and investors are more likely to invest in a country whose economy is doing well. As a result, in order to acquire such assets, you must buy that nation's currency.

Trend Reversal

When a market that has been rising, with higher highs and lower lows, starts to fall, this is known as a reversal. Conversely, a market in a downward trend indicates that it is about to turn around when it starts to make higher highs and higher lows.

When the direction of a currency pair's price shifts, it is called a trend reversal. For example, it might be considered a trend reversal if the price has been moving higher and suddenly begins to move lower. Depending on the time period they are utilizing, traders will interpret trend reversal differently.

Prediction and leveraging market trends are the two main components of forex trading. Making effective trades in the foreign currency market requires the ability to recognize a shift in trend. Traders may control their risk and decide when to enter or leave transactions by recognizing changes in the trend.

Being able to see a trend reversal early on might be the difference between a profitable trade and a losing one. Additionally, being able to distinguish between a true trend reversal and something more transient, like pullbacks, can have an impact on your potential to turn a profit because misleading signals are common in the forex market and being able to recognize them might influence your trading decisions.

Breakout

At this point, range-bound movements are transformed into distinct upward or negative trends when the market breaks its level of inertia. The underlying currency pair's velocity determines the possible shapes for the breakout stage.

Any price movement outside of a designated support or resistance level is referred to as a breakout.

Depending on the price action pattern, either a horizontal or diagonal level may see the breakout.

Using Trend Lines

Traders frequently utilize trend lines as tools, and plotting them on a chart makes it easy to see when a trend is about to revers. Trend lines can be diagonal or horizontal, and they will act as levels of support and resistance to help detect reversal signs.

First, two trend lines should be drawn. Two or more high price points can be connected to create the upper trend line, and two or more low price points can be connected to create the lower trend line. The trading platform has an indicator called trend lines that may be used to link the most important price points on the screen automatically, saving you time.

The price must breach either the upper or lower trend line as it begins to move in the other direction for there to be a trend reversal. An uptrend reversal is likely, for instance, if there is a breakout with lower highs and lower lows. A reversal of the downtrend is occurring when there are higher highs and lower lows. However, a breakout from a trend line may not always indicate that the trend is ending, and additional forex indicators may be needed to verify the reversal.

CHAPTER FIVE

TOP TREND TRADING STRATEEGY

Breakout Strategy in Trading

When the price breaks out of its range, a breakout strategy seeks to enter the transaction. Strong momentum is what traders seek, and the breakout itself serves as a signal to enter a position and take advantage of the next market action.

Traders may place buy-stop and sell-stop orders, or they may take positions in the market, in which case they will need to actively watch the price movement. Usually, they will set the stop slightly above or below the previous support or resistance level. Traders can utilize traditional levels of support and resistance to determine their exit goals.

It's a good idea to understand the degrees of support and resistance before moving forward. It will be much easier to see the price breakout from those levels if you are aware of it.

Degree Of Support

A chart over time will reveal certain support levels if you use technical analysis to trade. These are regions or particular levels where prices are often supported.

Support levels offer what is referred to as a price "floor." This indicates that prices often remain at this level because customers support them.

Degree Of Resistance

The antithesis of a support level is a resistance level.

Resistance levels are regions or levels on a chart where prices are often stopped (resisted) and are unable to rise further for a while.

Breakout Entry

Using the breakout entry to enter a trade when the price breaks through a resistance level is one strategy. Many traders believe that the price has the momentum to move higher when it breaks through the barrier level.

The idea behind this is that traders who see a breach of resistance may be positive and will encourage the price to rise.

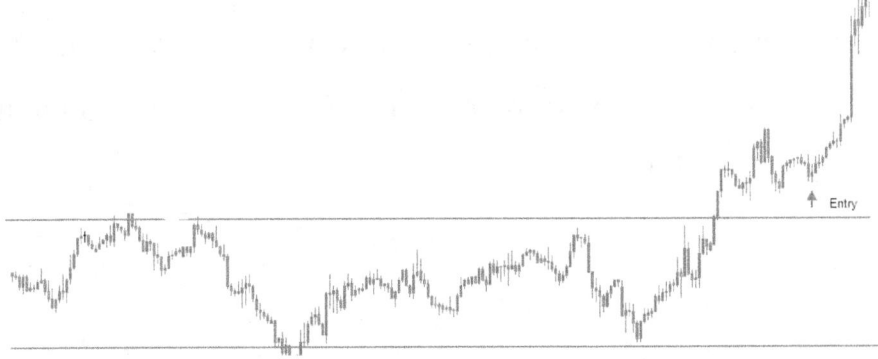

Many traders utilize this breakthrough from a resistance level as an entry point, albeit this may not always be the case.

Conversely, in the event that the price breaks through a support level, you might employ the breakout entry. A breach of support is typically interpreted as a warning that prices might decline much further. This breach of support is used by certain traders to profit from price declines.

You may utilize this entry approach for trading if you understand what support and resistance levels are and how to use them to determine when prices are breaking out of these levels.

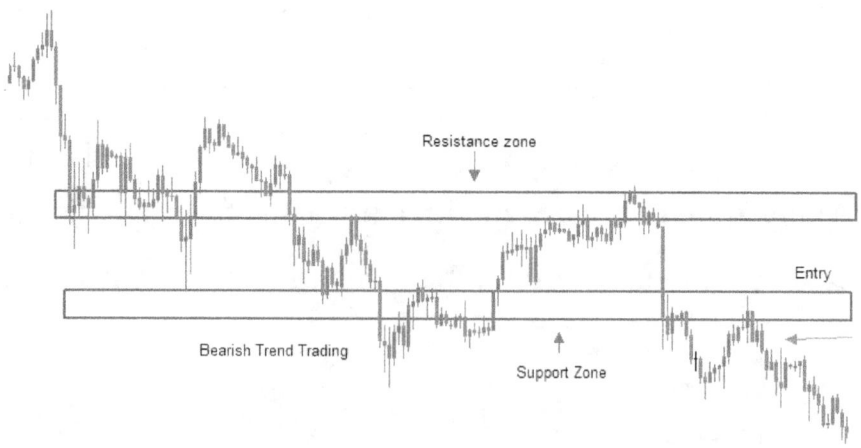

The MT4 trading platform's charting feature may be used to determine support and resistance levels whether you're using a real or demo trading account. Attempting to determine the support and resistance levels on various instruments at various times is also a very good idea.

It may be lot simpler for you to recognize any price breakouts after you are comfortable with and knowledgeable about these levels.

Confirming A Breakout

Trading a breakout may be as simple as placing a buy-stop or sell-stop order above or below the important support and resistance levels.

Because there is a greater likelihood that the breakout you are trading is a fake one, it is also considerably riskier. Since the price only stays above or below the important resistance/support level for relatively brief periods of time, false breakouts are common.

Because of the brakes being activated, there may be some initial momentum, but if there is not enough power behind the move, this momentum might disappear fast.

Traders can employ many techniques to verify the validity of a breakthrough. Keeping an eye on price action is the first step. This may work for you if you are a day trader because you are probably already in front of the monitor. Additionally, you have the option to set up an alert that will sound when the price approaches the target you have selected.

To choose whether or not the breakthrough seems legitimate to you, but you'll need the abilities and self-assurance. The deal might then be manually entered, but if the price changes too rapidly, you run the danger of missing the entire move.

Waiting for a pullback is an additional strategy. The price will frequently retest a critical resistance or support level after breaking above or below it. You might utilize this as an entry opportunity if the price rebounds off the previous resistance level or pauses ahead of the previous support level, which indicates that the breakout was legitimate. You run the danger of missing the major move, though, if the momentum has already slowed down by then.

It is possible to make money trading breakouts. However, there is a significant chance of a false breakout, which is why having a solid risk management strategy is crucial. Additionally, you want to strive for a risk/reward ratio that is at least 1:2.

One can trade breakouts at any time frame. A breakdown below a multi-year support level might be traded, and you could hold the trade for several months.

Breakout trading is more common among short-term traders, though, since they aim to capitalize on swift market movements that happen in a little amount of time. Trading on the lower time frames instead of the higher time frames makes it much easier to gain a sense of the market and its momentum.

Counter Trend Trading Strategy

A correction in an asset's price that goes against the primary trend is known as a counter trend. Put simply, a retreat to the downside in the market during an upswing is referred to as a countertrend as it deviates from the initial market trend.

A countertrend trading technique is an effort to enter a transaction against the primary trend in the hopes of making a tiny profit.

Assuming that there would be reversals or pullbacks in the present market trend, counter trend trading is a type of swing trading that aims to benefit from the pullback while the underlying trend persists. Positions are held using this medium-term technique for a few days or weeks.

Pullbacks are used by certain traders who utilize this profit-making method while keeping their primary positions moving in the trend's direction. Countertrend methods employ candlestick patterns, support and resistance levels, and momentum indicators to pinpoint potential entry positions into the market. Traders employing this strategy must be cautious though, since the present trend might suddenly restart at any point. Therefore, in order to minimize losses when trading this approach, appropriate risk management strategies such stop loss orders and minimum position sizes should be applied.

A trader who uses countertrend trading, a contrarian trading strategy, aims to make money from price movements that defy the dominant trend. Countertrend traders usually try to catch a short-term price pullback or even a trend reversal by fading the trend.

Countertrend trading techniques often have an intermediate time horizon. Countertrend swing traders especially aim to maintain positions for a few days to a few weeks. Additionally, there is a subset of short-term traders that use countertrend trading tactics and for whom this period may not be relevant. With their countertrend strategies, these day traders and scalpers can be in and out in a few hours or by the conclusion of the trading session.

That being said, the fundamental idea behind countertrend trading may be thought of as the antithesis of a trend-following approach. A contrarian or countertrend trading method frequently involves identifying prospective reversal points within the overall price movement, whereas a trend trading style concentrates on momentum breakouts and riding a trend for as long as feasible.

A trend trader's perspective differs greatly from a contrarian trader. Both trading approaches have the potential to be successful when the market conditions and a trader's psychological and personal characteristics are met.

The following actions should be taken while trading forex counter-trend:

- Determine the Market Trend: The first step in counter-trend trading is to determine the current market trend. Technical analysis methods like trend lines, chart patterns, and moving averages can be used for this.
- Determine Important Levels of Support and Resistance: After determining the direction of the

market, you must determine important levels of support and resistance.

Technical analysis methods like trend lines, moving averages, and Fibonacci retracements can be used to identify these levels.

- Await confirmation - Prior to entering a trade, ensure that there is proof of a market reversal. Finding price action indicators, like as momentum indicators, chart patterns, and candlestick patterns, can help with this.

- Take the Trade: Move into the position as soon as you have proof that the market is turning around. To control your risk, be careful to establish your take-profit and stop-loss thresholds.

Although it may be extremely dangerous, countertrend trading can also be quite rewarding. Here are a few success strategies:

- Employ Appropriate Risk Management - Trading against the trend can be dangerous, therefore it's critical to employ appropriate risk management strategies, such as determining take-profit and stop-loss levels.

- Use different Time Frames: It's critical to validate the reversal while trading countertrend by using different time frames. Your trade accuracy can rise and erroneous signals can be decreased as a result.

- Keep an Eye on the News - Events and news in the market may have a big influence on forex prices, therefore it's critical to monitor the news and modify your trading strategy as necessary.

- Avoid Overtrading - While it may be alluring to trade against the trend, it's crucial to avoid going overboard. Adhere to your trading strategy and only enter trades when there is a good chance of winning.

Trading With the Actual Trend

Following the trend equates to going with the flow.

Why would you want to search for short entry when purchasing might lead to more easier transactions when the overall trend is upward?

Even in situations when there is a clear trend, a lot of novice traders continue to try to forecast reversals and burn their fingers going against the trend, when they might have earned far more money by just following the trend.

However, you may still include the idea of trading with the trend and with momentum into your standard trading strategy even if you are not a trend-following trader. An essential trading talent is the ability to predict where the price will go and which side of the market is stronger.

In trend trading, profits are realized by observing an asset's momentum as it moves in a certain direction, such as up, down, or sideways.

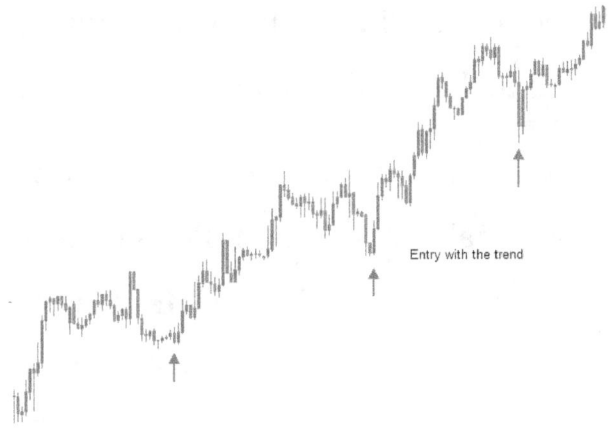

Entry with the trend

Trend trading may be compared to following the path of least resistance; if the market is rising, you would go long, and if it is dropping, you would go short.

Distinguishing trends into primary and secondary movements is helpful. A principal trend delineates the enduring, comprehensive trend. However, there are also secondary trends, which are sporadic variations.

Consequently, you may be a swing trader in a trending market by betting on the smaller peaks and troughs, even if some trend traders will adopt a wider stance.

Using a tried-and-true method called trend trading, traders aim to make money by following the direction of the trend and holding onto their positions until it shifts.

For this technique to be profitable, the market price patterns that are in place must be followed. While prices are rising higher, trend traders will take a long position; while prices are trending downward, they will take a short position.

Technical indicators are a common tool used by trend traders to determine trends and determine when to enter and exit trades.

Moving averages and moving average convergence divergence (MACD) indicators are the most often utilized indicators. Because they depict price movements without being too late to identify changes in direction or momentum, moving average indicators are widely used. Because the crossings in MACD indicators occasionally signal the start of a trend shift, they can be useful.

Based on the current trend, trend traders take a position and maintain it until the trend changes or appears to be changing. One of the most crucial things to learn when starting out in forex trading is how to recognize trends. Upon comprehending the factors that propel trends and recognizing them, you may utilize this knowledge to enhance your trading choices.

The apparent inclination of financial markets to move in a specific way over time is known as a market trend. For long time periods, these movements are categorized as secular, for medium and short time periods, as main and secondary. Technical analysis, a framework that describes market trends as predictable price tendencies within the market when the price approaches support and resistance levels, altering over time, is used by traders to try to discover market trends.

A trend trader, therefore, seeks out circumstances in which the velocity of price movement is greater in one direction than the other (i.e., upward or downward). These traders may stick onto their holdings for weeks or months at a period, or they may take on extremely short-term bets (scalping) to profit from tiny price swings.

GET INSTANT ACCESS TO THE FREE VIDEO COURSE BY FOLLOWING THE BELOW LINK

subscribepage.io/freeforexcourse

Click or copy and paste the above link on your browser for instant access to the bonus video.

Happy Trading!

www.ingramcontent.com/pod-product-compliance
Lightning Source LLC
Chambersburg PA
CBHW062258290526
45794CB00006B/2607